# Aaron and Gayla's Alphabet Book

**Acknowledgments**
*Aaron and Gayla's Alphabet Book.* Text copyright © 1993 by Eloise Greenfield. Illustrations copyright © 1993 by Jan Spivey Gilchrist. Reprinted by arrangement with Black Butterfly Children's Books/Writers and Readers Publishing, Inc.

Photography
**31** Jose L. Pelaez/The Stock Market  **32** Dave Bradly; (background) Patrick Ramsey/International Stock  **33** Dave Bradly; (background) Andy Sacks/Tony Stone Images  **34** George Disario/The Stock Market  **35** SuperStock  **36** Dave Bradly **37** Courtesy of Eloise Greenfield

Houghton Mifflin Edition, 2005
Copyright © 2001 by Houghton Mifflin Company. All rights reserved.

PRINTED IN CHINA

ISBN: 978-0-618-03641-7

ISBN: 0-618-03641-5

18 19-0940-10

# Aaron and Gayla's Alphabet Book

**pictures by Jan Spivey Gilchrist**
**written by Eloise Greenfield**

HOUGHTON MIFFLIN   BOSTON • MORRIS PLAINS, NJ

California • Colorado • Georgia • Illinois • New Jersey • Texas

# Aa

**My name is Aaron.**

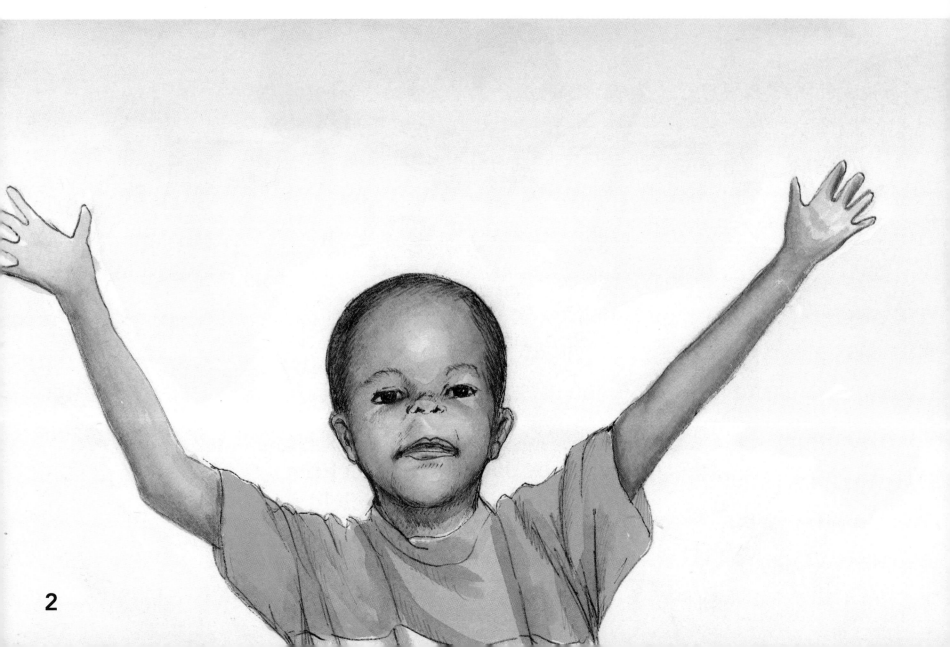

# B b

**I sit beside the window.**

3

# Cc

**I drive my car.**

4

# Dd

I dig a hole.

# Ee

I eat my dinner.

# Ff

I look **for a** friend.

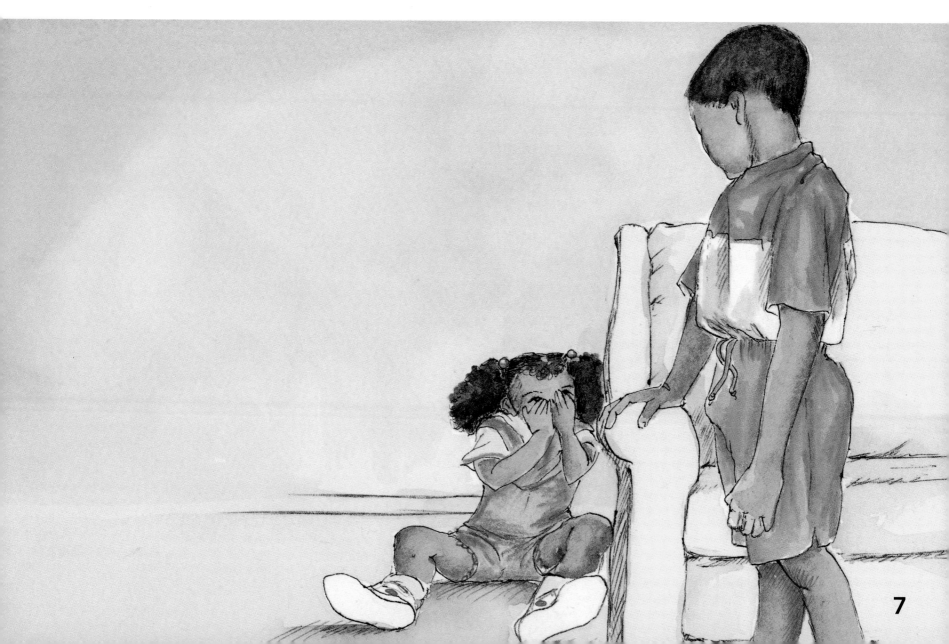

# Gg

**My name is Gayla.**

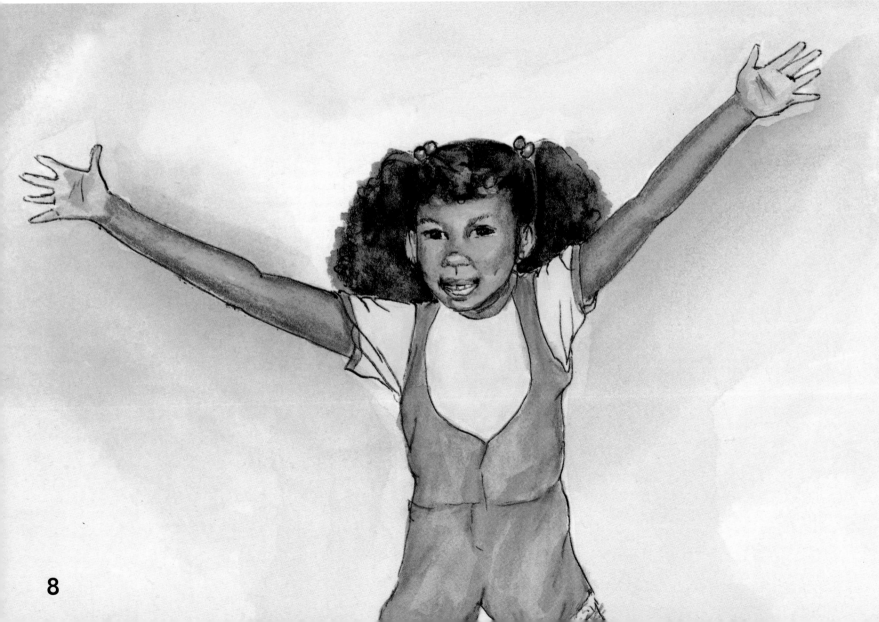

# Hh

I hide **my toys under the bed.**

# Ii

I look in the big hole.

# J j

I jump over the puddle.

# Kk

I kick the ball.

# Ll

I look for a friend.

# Mm

We meet.

# Nn

**We make noise.**

# Oo

We open an old box.

# Pp

We play together.

# We quarrel.

# Rr

## We run.

# Ss
**We** sit **beside each other.**

# Tt

## We play together.

# Uu We look under the bed.

# Vv

**We** visit **the teddy bear.**

# Ww

**We play together.**

# Xx

**We x-ray the teddy bear.**

# Yy

We yawn.

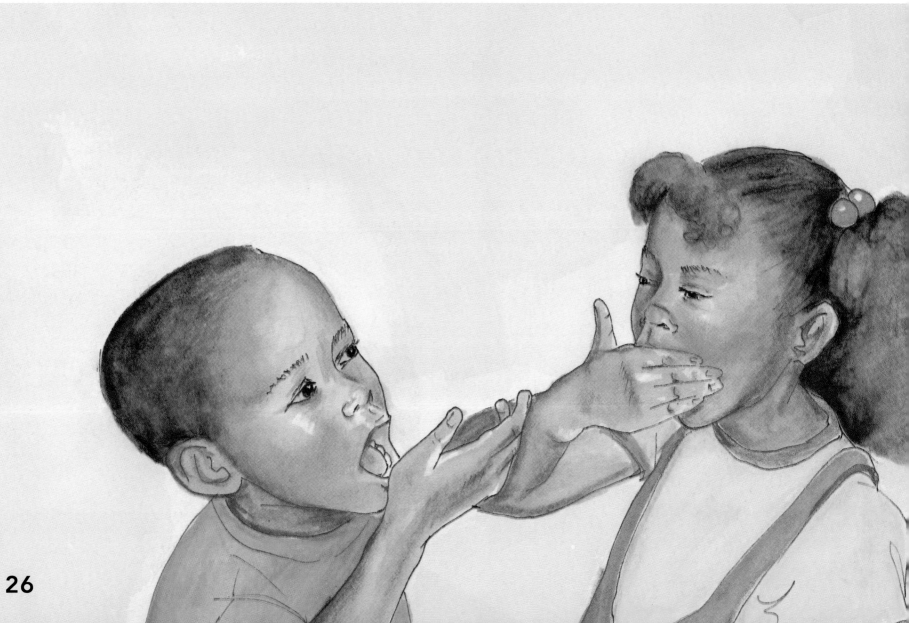

26

# Zz

We snore. Zzzzzz.

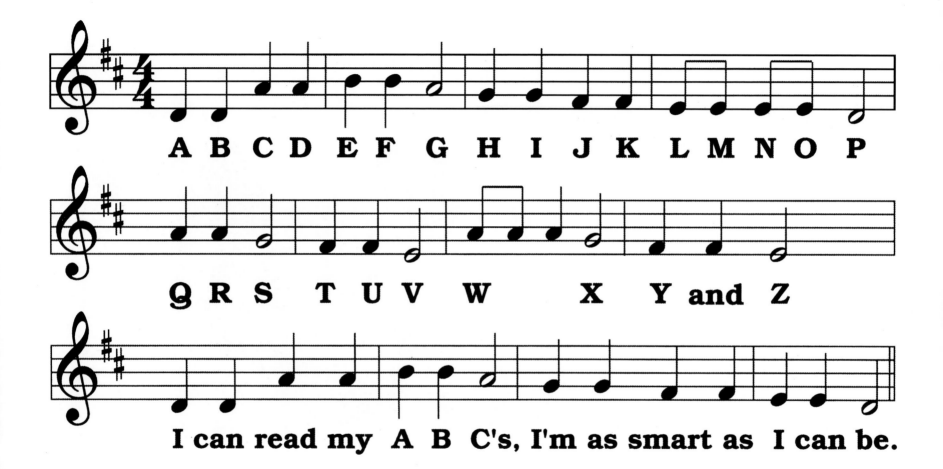

ABCDEF GHI JK LMNOP

QRS TUV W X Y and Z

I can read my A B C's, I'm as smart as I can be.

# We Read Together

# We read a grocery list.

# We read a magazine.

# We read a newspaper.

# We read a menu.

# We read a book . . .

by Eloise Greenfield.
And here she is!